T0063784

The School of Life:
On Being Nice

The School of Life:
On Being Nice

A guide to friendship and connection

The School of Life

First published in 2017 by The School of Life
First published in the USA in 2018
This paperback edition published in 2022
930 High Road, London, N12 9RT

© The School of Life 2017

Designed and typeset by Marcia Mihotich
Printed and bound in Canada

All rights reserved. This book is sold subject to the condition
that it shall not be resold, lent, hired out, or otherwise circulated
without express prior consent of the publisher.
A proportion of this book has appeared online at
www.theschooloflife.com/thebookoflife

Every effort has been made to contact the copyright holders
of the material reproduced in this book. If any have been
inadvertently overlooked, the publisher will be pleased to make
restitution at the earliest opportunity.

The School of Life is a resource for helping us understand
ourselves, for improving our relationships, our careers, and our
social lives—as well as for helping us find calm and get more
out of our leisure hours. We do this through creating films,
workshops, books, apps, and gifts.

www.theschooloflife.com

ISBN 978-1-915087-15-7

10 9 8 7 6 5 4 3 2 1

Contents

1
Why We Don't Really Want to Be Nice

Setting out to try to become a nicer person sounds like a deeply colorless and dispiriting ambition. In theory, we love niceness, but in practice, the concept appears to be embarrassingly anodyne, meek, tedious, and even sexless. Being a nice person sounds like something we would try to be only after every other more arduous and more rewarding alternative had failed.

Our suspicion of niceness may feel personal, but it has a long history, bearing the sediment of at least four major cultural currents that we should try to understand:

i.

The Legacy of Christianity: Nice but Weak

For centuries, Christianity was the single most powerful force shaping our intellectual horizons, and it was profoundly committed to promoting niceness to the world. With the finest aesthetic and intellectual resources, it sang the praises of forgiveness, charity, tenderness, and empathy.

But—unfortunately for niceness—Christianity didn't simply leave it there. It also suggested that there might be a fundamental opposition between being nice and being successful. Successful people, believers were told, were not, on the whole, very nice people—and nice people were not, on the whole, very successful. It seemed that applicants to the Kingdom of Heaven had a choice to make: niceness or success.

This dichotomy deeply tarnished the appeal of niceness to anyone with the faintest spark of healthy, worldly ambition in their hearts. Christianity might have been striving to enthuse people about niceness, but by connecting it up so firmly with failure, it created an enduring feeling that this quality was chiefly of interest to losers.

ii.

The Legacy of Romanticism:
Nice but Boring

For the last 200 years, we have been heavily influenced by the cultural movement known as Romanticism. For the Romantics, the admirable person has been synonymous with the exciting person: someone intense and creative, mercurial and spontaneous; someone who might upset tradition and dare to be forceful, or even rude, while following the call of their own heart.

The diametric opposite of this heroic figure was, for the Romantics, someone mild and respectable, guarded and conservative, unflashy and quiet: in other words, the boring person. Here, too, there has seemed a radical choice to be made: either fiery, unpredictable, and brilliant or meek, conventional, and in bed by 9 p.m.

iii.

The Legacy of Capitalism:
Nice but Bankrupt

To this charge sheet of niceness, capitalism added another indictment, presenting an interpretation of the world as a deeply competitive arena in which all companies were committed to forge continuous battle for market share, in an atmosphere marked by ruthlessness, determination, and impatience. Those who succeeded had to know how to destroy the competition and handle the workforce without a trace of emotion. A nice person, unwilling to squeeze wages or outwit an opponent, would end up either bankrupt or in the mailroom.

iv.
The Legacy of Eroticism:
Nice but Unsexy

A final, more personal, association hangs over niceness: the belief that the nice can't be sexually desirable, because the qualities that make us sexy are bound up with the possession of brutal, domineering, confident edges at odds with the tenderness and coziness of the nice. Once again, an awkward choice presents itself: between the pleasant friend with whom to go to the park and the dangerous companion with whom to disappear into the dungeon.

Despite all this, the truth is that we like niceness very much and depend upon it even more. It is just that our true memories of niceness have been suppressed by a culture that unfairly makes us feel unintelligent for lending niceness our approval. All of the qualities we have been taught to think of as opposed to niceness are in fact highly compatible with and, at points, highly dependent upon it.

However much we are committed to success, for long portions of our lives we are intensely vulnerable creatures wholly at the mercy of the gentleness of others. We are only ever able to be successful because other people—usually our mothers—have given up a good share of their lives to being nice to us.

As for excitement, this too can only be a phase,

as all those who have ever made real contributions to humankind know. Quiet days, domestic routine, and regular bedtimes are the necessary preconditions of creative highs. There is nothing more sterile than a demand that life be constantly exciting.

For its part, capitalism may reward competition between firms, but it relies on collaboration within them. No company can function long without trust and bonds of personal affection. Much to the frustration of bosses, money cannot guarantee the commitment required from employees in all the more sophisticated areas of the economy; only meaning and a spirit of companionship will.

Lastly, the sexual thrill of nastiness only ever properly entices in conditions of trust. However much we may fantasize about a night with a ruthless conqueror, it would be alarming to wind up with an actual example. We need to know that someone is fundamentally kind before an offer of a rope and the sound of swear words become properly interesting.

So much of what we value is in fact preserved by niceness and is compatible with it. We can be nice and successful; nice and exciting; nice and wealthy; and nice and potent. Niceness is a virtue awaiting our rediscovery and our renewed, unconflicted appreciation.

2
Kindness

i.
Charity

At its most basic, charity means offering someone something they need but can't get for themselves. That is normally understood to mean something material; we overwhelmingly associate charity with giving money.

The heroes of Christianity are exemplars of such charity. Outside the city, St Francis comes across a poor man. His garments are thin and ragged. Winter is coming on and coats are expensive. The saint is moved to charity and hands over his cloak.

But, at its core, charity goes far beyond finance. It is in our relations with colleagues, friends, and family members that charity becomes particularly necessary. Here what we tend to be short of is *charity of interpretation:* that is, a kindly perspective on the weaknesses, eccentricities, anxieties, and follies that we present but are unable to win direct sympathy for.

A charitable soul does the extra work for us. They come forward with explanations of why we behave as we do: They understand enough about our past to have a picture of where our impatience or over-ambition, rashness or meekness comes from. They hold in mind what happened with our parents and with the move to another country. They create a picture of who the person in the "begging" position is that is sufficiently generous and complex as to make us more than just the "fool" or "weirdo," the "failure" or "loser" that we might otherwise so easily have been dismissed as.

The genuinely charitable person gives generously from a sense that they too will stand in need of charity. Not right now, not over this, but in some other area. They know that self-righteousness is merely the result of a faulty memory, an inability to hold in mind—at moments when one is truly good and totally in the right—how often one has been deeply and definitively in the wrong.

Charity remembers how there might still be virtue amid much evil. Charity keeps in mind that if someone is tired and stressed, they are liable to behave appallingly. Charity is aware that when someone shouts an insult, they are not usually revealing the secret truth about their feelings; they are trying to wound the other because they feel they have been hurt—usually by someone else who they don't have the authority to injure back.

Charity is interested in mitigating circumstances, in parts of the truth that can cast a less catastrophic light on our follies.

In financial matters, charity tends to flow in one direction. The philanthropist may be very generous, but usually they stay rich; they are habitually the giver rather than the recipient. But in life as a whole, and especially in relationships, charity is unlikely to end up one-sided: Who is weak and who is powerful can change rapidly and frequently. You are likely to be, as it were, a "patron" in one area and a "beggar" in another. So, we must be kind not only because we are touched by the suffering of others but because we properly understand that we are never too far from being in need of an equally vital dose of charity to get through life.

ii.
The Weakness of Strength

In our efforts to be kind, it can help to consider a theory known as the Weakness of Strength. The failings of friends, colleagues, and partners can be deeply galling. We become close to them because of their skills and merits, but after a while it can be the disappointing sides of their personalities that dominate our view of them.

We look upon their faults and wonder why they are the way they are. Why so slow? Why so unreliable? How can they be so bad at explaining things or telling an anecdote? Why can't they face bad news straight on? Even worse, we feel they *could* change—if only they really wanted to; if only they weren't so mean ...

The Weakness of Strength theory dictates that we should strive to see people's weaknesses as the inevitable downside of certain merits that drew us to them, and from which we will benefit at other points, even if these benefits are not apparent right now. What we are seeing are not their faults, pure and simple, but rather the shadow side of things that are genuinely good about them. We're picking up on weaknesses that derive from strengths. If we were to write down a list of strengths and then of weaknesses, we'd find that almost everything on the positive side could be connected with something on the negative side.

In the 1870s, when he was living in Paris, the American novelist Henry James became a good friend of the celebrated Russian novelist Ivan Turgenev, who was also living in the city at that time. Henry James was particularly taken by the unhurried, tranquil style of the Russian writer's storytelling. He obviously took a long time over every sentence, weighing different options, changing and polishing, until everything was perfect. It was an ambitious, inspiring approach to writing.

But in personal and social life, these same virtues could make Turgenev a maddening companion. He'd accept an invitation to lunch; then—the day before—send a note explaining that he would be unable to attend; then another saying how much he looked forward to the occasion. Then he would turn up, two hours late. Arranging anything with him was a nightmare, yet his social waywardness was really just the same thing that made him so attractive as a writer. It was the same unwillingness to hurry, the same desire to keep the options open until the last moment.

This produced marvelous books—and dinner party chaos. In reflecting on Turgenev's character, Henry James remarked that his Russian friend was exhibiting the "weakness of his strength."

The theory goes like this: Every strength that an individual has brings with it a weakness of which it is an inherent part. It is impossible to have strengths without weaknesses. *Every virtue has an associated weakness.* Not all the virtues can belong together in a single person.

This is a theory that can help calm us down at moments of particular crisis, because it changes the way we see the defects, failings, and weaknesses of others. Our minds tend to hive off the strengths and see these as essential while deeming the weaknesses as a freakish add-on, but, in truth, the weaknesses are part and parcel of the strengths.

This theory usefully undermines the unhelpful idea that, if only we looked a bit harder, we would find someone who was always perfect to be around. If strengths are invariably connected to failings, there won't be anyone who is remotely flawless. We may well find people with different strengths, but they will also have a new litany of weaknesses. It is always calming to take a moment to remind ourselves that perfect people don't exist.

iii.
Losers and Tragic Heroes

Our societies are very interested in winners but don't really know what to do about losers—of which there are always, by definition, many more.

For a long time, around success and failure, the rhetoric tends to be very upbeat. We hear about resilience, bouncing back, never surrendering, and giving it another go. But there's only so long this kind of talk can go on. At some point, the conclusion becomes inevitable: Things won't work out. The political career is not going to have a comeback. There'll be no way of getting finance for the movie. The novel won't be accepted by the 32nd publisher. The criminal charges will always taint one's reputation.

Where does responsibility for success and failure lie? Nowadays, the answer tends to be: squarely with the individual concerned. That is why failure is not only hard (and it always has been), but a catastrophe. There is no metaphysical consolation, no possibility of appealing to an idea of "bad luck," no one to blame but oneself. No wonder suicide rates climb exponentially once societies modernize and start to hold people responsible for their biographies. Meritocracies turn failure from a misfortune into an unbudgeable verdict on one's nature.

But not all societies and eras have seen success and failure in such a stark light. In Ancient Greece, another remarkable possibility—quite ignored by our own era—was envisaged: You could be good and yet fail. To keep this idea at the front of the collective imagination, the Ancient Greeks developed a particular art form: tragic drama. They put on huge festivals, which all citizens were expected to attend, to act out stories of appalling, often grisly, failure. People were seen to break a minor law, or make a hasty decision, or sleep with the wrong person, and the result was ignominy and death. What happened was shown to be to a large extent in the hands of what the Greeks called "fate" or "the Gods." It was the Greeks' poetic way of saying that things often work out in random ways, according to dynamics that don't reflect the merits of the individuals concerned.

In *The Poetics*, the philosopher Aristotle (384–322 BCE) defined the key ingredients of tragedy. The hero of the tragedy should be a decent person: "better than average," often high-born but prone to making small mistakes. At the start, it may not be obvious that they are making an error. But by an unfortunate chain of events, for which they are not wholly to blame, this small mistake leads to a catastrophe.

Tragedy is the sympathetic, morally complex, account of how good people can end up in disastrous situations. It is the very opposite of today's tabloid newspapers or social media, where the mob rushes to make judgments on those who have slipped up. Aristotle thought it extremely important that people see tragic works on a regular basis to counter their otherwise strong inclinations to judge and moralize. Aristotle thought a good tragedy should inspire both pity and fear: pity for the tragic hero based on an understanding of how easy it is to make the slip that leads to disaster; and fear for oneself as one realizes how open our lives are to careering out of control. All of us could quite quickly come apart if ever events chose to test us.

Tragedy is meant to be a corrective to easy judgment. It exists to counter our natural instincts to admire only the successful, to spurn those who fail, and to dismiss unfortunates as losers.

We are currently uncomfortable around the idea of a good person not succeeding. We'd rather say that they weren't good than embrace a far more disturbing and less well-publicized thought: that the world is very unfair. But without the idea of tragedy, we make existence for everyone far crueller and more judgmental than it need be.

iv.
Motives

A fundamental path to remaining calm and kind around people, even in very challenging situations, is being able to distinguish between what someone does and what they meant to do. In law, the difference is enshrined in the contrasting concepts of murder and manslaughter. The result may be the same; the body is inert in a pool of blood. But we collectively feel it makes a huge difference what the perpetrator's intentions were.

We care about intentions for a very good reason: If the action was deliberate, then the perpetrator will be a persistent source of danger from whom the community must be protected. But if it was accidental, then the perpetrator will be inclined to deep apology and restitution, which renders punishment and rage far less necessary. Picture yourself in a restaurant where the waiter has spilt a glass of wine on your laptop. The damage is severe, and your rage starts to mount. But whether this was an accident or a willing strategy is key to an appropriate response. A concerted desire to spill signals that the waiter needs to be confronted head-on. You may have to take radical, defensive steps, like shouting at them or calling for help. But if it was an accident, then the person isn't your enemy. There's no need to swear at them. In fact, it makes a lot of sense to be forgiving and kindly, because benevolence will imminently be heading your way.

Motives are therefore crucial. Unfortunately, we are seldom good at perceiving what motives are involved in the incidents that hurt us. We are easily and wildly mistaken. We see intention where there was none and escalate and confront when no strenuous or agitated responses are warranted.

Part of the reason why we jump so readily to dark conclusions and see plots to insult and harm us is a rather poignant psychological phenomenon: self-hatred. The less we like ourselves, the more we appear in our own eyes as plausible targets for mockery and harm. Why would a drill have started up outside just as we were settling down to work? Why is the room service breakfast not arriving, even though we will have to be in a meeting very soon? Why would the phone operator be taking so long to find our details? Because there is, logically enough, a plot against us. Because we are appropriate targets for these kinds of things; because we are the sorts of people against whom disruptive drilling is legitimately likely to be directed; because it's what we deserve.

When we carry an excess of self-disgust around with us, operating just below the radar of conscious awareness, we constantly seek confirmation from the wider world that we really are the worthless people we take ourselves to be. The expectation is almost always set in childhood, where someone close to us is likely to have left us feeling dirty and culpable. As a result, we now travel through society assuming the worst, not because it is necessarily true (or pleasant) to do so, but because it feels familiar; because we are the prisoners of past patterns we haven't yet understood.

Small children sometimes behave in stunningly unfair ways: They scream at the person looking after them, angrily push away a bowl of animal pasta, throw away something you have just fetched for them. But we rarely feel personally agitated or wounded by their behavior, because we don't assign a negative motive or mean intention to a small person. We reach around for the most benevolent interpretations. We don't think they are doing it in order to upset us. We probably think that they are getting tired, or their gums are sore, or they are upset by the arrival of a younger sibling. We have a large repertoire of alternative explanations ready in our heads, none of which leads us to panic or become agitated.

This is the reverse of what tends to happen around adults. Here we imagine that people have deliberately got us in their sights. If someone edges in front of us in the airport queue, it's natural to suppose they have sized us up and reasoned that they can safely take advantage of us. They probably relish the thought of causing us a little distress. But if we employed the infant model of interpretation, our first assumption would be quite different: maybe they didn't sleep well last night and are too exhausted to think straight; maybe they've got a sore knee; maybe they are doing the equivalent of testing the boundaries of parental tolerance: Is jumping in front of someone in the queue playing the same role as peeing in the garden? Seen from such a point of view, the adult's behavior doesn't magically become nice or acceptable. But the level of agitation is kept safely low. It's very touching that we live in a world where we have learned to be so kind to children; it would be even nicer if we learned to be more generous towards the childlike parts of one another.

The French philosopher Émile-Auguste Chartier (known as Alain; 1868–1951) was said to be the finest teacher in France in the first half of the 20th century. He developed a formula for calming himself and his pupils down in the face of irritating people. "Never say that people are evil," he wrote. "You just need to look for the pin." What he meant was: look for the source of the agony that drives a person to behave in appalling ways. The calming thought is to imagine that they are suffering off-stage, in some area we cannot see. To be mature is to learn to imagine this zone of pain, in spite of the lack of available evidence. They may not look as if they were maddened by an inner psychological ailment; they may look chirpy and full of themselves. But the "pin" simply must be there, or they would not be causing us harm.

Chartier was drawing on one of the great techniques of literary fiction: the ability to take us into the mind of a character—perhaps a very unglamorous or initially off-putting figure—and show us the powerful, but unexpected, things going on in their mind. It was a move a novelist like Fyodor Dostoevsky (1821–1881) was deeply excited by: He would take the kinds of characters that his readers would normally dismiss with a shudder—an outcast, a criminal, a gambler—and describe the complex depths of their inner lives, their capacity for remorse, their hopes and their powers of sensitive perception.

This move—the accurate, corrective, reimagining of the inner lives of others—is relevant far outside the realm of literary fiction. It's a piece of empathetic reflection that we constantly need to perform with ourselves and with others. We need to imagine the turmoil, disappointment, worry, and sadness in people who may outwardly appear merely aggressive. We need to aim compassion in an unexpected place: at those who annoy us most.

V.

Suffering and Meanness

It happens pretty much all the time: a small jabbing comment, a joke at our expense amid a group of old friends, a line of sarcasm, a sneering assessment, a provocative comment on the internet.

These things hurt a lot—more than we're ever allowed to admit. In the privacy of our minds, we search for explanations, but anything satisfying and soothing is usually hard to come by. We're just left to puzzle at the casual inhumanity that circulates all around us and suspect that it's we who are somehow to blame for falling victim to it.

This is what we should actually think—a truth as basic as it is inviolable: Other people have been nasty because they are in pain. The only reason they have hurt us is because they are—somewhere deep inside—hurting themselves. They have been catty and derogatory and foul because they are not well. However outwardly confident they may look, however virile and robust they may appear, their actions are all the evidence we need that they cannot be in a good place. No one solid would ever need to do this.

The thought is empowering because nastiness so readily humiliates and reduces us. It turns us into the small, damaged party. Without meaning to, we begin to imagine our bully as potent and even somehow impressive. Their vindictiveness demeans us. But the psychological explanation of evil at once reverses the power dynamic. It is you who has no need to belittle, who is in fact the larger, steelier, more forceful party; it is you—who feels so defenseless—who is actually in power.

The thought restores justice. It promises that the guilty party has, after all, been punished along the way. You might not have been able to right the scales personally (they had already left the room or kept the conversation flowing too fast for you to protest—and in any case, you're not the sort to make a fuss). But a kind of punishment has been delivered cosmically already somewhere behind the scenes; their suffering, of which their need to inflict suffering on others is incontrovertible evidence, is all you need to know that they have been served their just desserts. You move from being a victim of crime to being an audience to an abstract form of justice. They may not be apologizing to you, but they haven't escaped freely either; their sulfur is proof that they pay a heavy price.

This is not merely a pleasant story. A person who feels at ease with themselves can have no need to distress others. We don't have the energy to be cruel unless, and until, we are in inner torment.

Along the way, this theory gives hints at how we might—when we have recovered from the blow—deal with those who dealt it. The temptation is to be stern and cruel back, but the only way to diminish the vicious cycle of hate is to address its origins, which lie in suffering. There is no point punching back. We must—as the old prophets always told us—learn to look upon our enemies with sorrow, pity, and, when we can manage it, a forgiving kind of love.

vi.
Politeness

For most of human history, the idea of being "polite" has been central to our sense of what is required to count as a good and civilized person. But more recently, politeness has come under suspicion. While we may not reject it outright, it's not a word we instinctively reach for when we want to explain why we like or admire someone. "Politeness" can sometimes even carry almost the opposite of its traditional connotations, suggesting an offensive or insolent degree of insincerity and inauthenticity. A "polite" person may be judged as a bit fake—and in their own way, really rather rude.

The rise in our collective suspicion of politeness has a history. Politeness used to be a key virtue for young aristocrats, yet by the late 18th century it had been thrown into disrepute. An alternative, Romantic ideal had emerged, in large part driven by the Swiss philosopher Jean-Jacques Rousseau (1712–1778), who powerfully redescribed politeness as an indication of servility and outright deceit. What was important for Rousseau was never to hide or moderate emotions and thoughts, but to remain—at all times—fundamentally true to oneself.

Rousseau's writings generated highly influential new ideals of behavior, to which we remain heirs. The Romantic suspicion of politeness was boosted further by the increasing role of the United States in global consciousness. Being direct and open came to be seen, by Americans themselves, as one of their chief national virtues—an attitude encapsulated in a climactic line from the 1939 movie *Gone with the Wind*, when Rhett Butler turns to Scarlett O'Hara and tells her exactly how he sees it ("Frankly my dear, I don't give a damn!"). And because America has been the world's most influential culture for around a century and a half, its attitude towards politeness has been widely and pervasively disseminated around the planet ever since.

What ultimately separates the Polite from the Frank person isn't really knowledge of etiquette. The difference doesn't hang upon considerations of which knife to use at a formal dinner, when to say "please" or "thank you" and how to word a wedding invitation. It comes down to a contrasting set of beliefs about human nature. The Polite and the Frank person behave differently chiefly because they see the world in highly divergent ways. These are some of the key ideological issues that separate them:

Purity vs. Sin

Frank people believe in the importance of expressing themselves honestly principally because they trust that what they think and feel will be fundamentally acceptable to the world. Their true sentiments and opinions may, when voiced, be bracing, but no worse. These Frank types assume that what is honestly avowed cannot ever be vindictive, disgusting, tedious, or cruel. In this sense, the Frank person sees themselves a little in the way we typically see small children: as blessed by an original and innate goodness.

Even the most etiquette conscious among us don't usually think that the strictures of politeness apply to the very young. We remain interested in whatever may be passing through these diminutive creatures' minds and stay unalarmed by their awkward moments, infelicities, or negative statements. If they say that the pasta is yuk or that the taxi driver has a head like a weird goldfish, it sounds funny rather than wounding. Their habit of addressing their stories to their teddy rather than to the adult sitting opposite them is just a touching sign of their free-spiritedness. It doesn't matter that there is a stain on their T-shirt when they meet a stranger. The Frank person taps into this childlike optimism in their own uninhibited approach to themselves. Their trust in their basic purity erodes the rationale for editing or self-censorship. They can believe that everything about them will more or less prove fine, whatever they happen to say or do.

The Polite person, by contrast, proceeds under a grave suspicion of themselves and their impulses. They sense that a great deal of what they feel and want isn't very nice. They are in touch with their darker desires and can sense their fleeting wishes to hurt or humiliate certain people. They know they are sometimes a bit revolting and cannot forget the extent to which they may be offensive and frightening to others. They therefore set out on a deliberate strategy to protect others from what they know is within them. It isn't lying as such. They merely understand that being "themselves" is a threat they must take enormous pains to spare everyone else from experiencing—especially anyone they claim to care about.

Paradoxically, the Polite person who is pessimistic about their own nature doesn't in fact end up behaving horribly with anyone. So aware are they of their own unlikable sides, they nimbly minimize their impact upon the world. It is their extraordinary suspicion of themselves that helps them be uncommonly friendly, trustworthy, and kind in everyday life.

The Stranger Is like Me vs. The Stranger Is Other

The Frank person operates with a charming unconscious assumption that other people are at heart pretty much like them; this can make them very clubbable and allows them to create some astonishing intimacies across social barriers at high speed. When they like listening to a particular piece of music at high volume, they will take it as obvious that you do as well. Because they are very enthusiastic about spicy food, or never want to add salt to a dish, it doesn't cross their mind to ask if you actually like this restaurant or would favor a salt cellar on the table. They can tell you about a bodily function or an aspect of their sex life without knowing you too well, because they have faith that we are all much the same in our emotions in these areas. They are correspondingly undisturbed by the less obvious clues about some of the dissonant feelings that may be unfolding in the minds of other people: If someone is quiet at a meeting, it doesn't occur to the Frank person to worry that they might have said something wrong or badly misjudged the situation.

For their part, the Polite person starts from the assumption that others are likely to be in quite different places internally, whatever the outward signs. Their behavior is therefore tentative, wary, and filled with enquiries. They will explicitly check up with others to take a measure of their experiences and outlook; if they feel cold, they are very alive to the possibility that you may be feeling perfectly warm and so will ask if you would mind if they closed the window. They are aware that you might be annoyed by a joke that they find funny or that you might hold sincere political opinions quite at odds with their own. They don't take what is going on for them as a guide to what might be going on for you. Their manners are grounded in an acute sense of the gulf that can separate humans from one another.

Robustness vs. Vulnerability

The Frank person works with an underlying sense that other people are for the most part extremely robust internally. Those around them are not felt to be forever on the verge of self-doubt and self-hatred. Their egos are not assumed to be gossamer thin and at perpetual risk of deflating. There is therefore understood to be no need to let out constant small signals of reassurance and affirmation. When you go to someone's house, the fact that the meal was tasty will be obvious to everyone, not least the person who spent four and a half hours cooking it. There is no need to keep stressing the point in a variety of discreet ways. When one meets an artist, there's no need to mention that their last work was noticed and appreciated; they'll know that well enough. And the office junior must have a pretty clear sense that they are making the grade without a need to stop and spell it out. The Frank person assumes that everyone's ego is already as big and strong as it should be. They are even likely to suspect that if you praise someone for the little things, you will only inflate their self-regard to undue and dangerous proportions.

The Polite person starts from a contrary assumption that all of us are permanently only millimeters away from inner collapse, despair, and self-hatred. However confident we may look, we are painfully vulnerable—

despite the outward plaudits and recognition—to a sense of being disliked and taken for granted. Every piece of neglect, every silence, or slightly harsh or off-the-cuff word has a profound capacity to hurt. All of us are walking around without a skin. The cook, the artist, and the office junior will inevitably share in a craving for evidence that what they do and are is OK. Accordingly, the Polite person will be drawn to spend a lot of time noticing and commenting positively on the most apparently minor facets of others' achievements: They will say that the watercress soup was the best they've had in years; they'll mention that the ending of the writer's new novel made them cry; they'll say that the work on the Mexico deal was helpful to, and noticed by, the whole company. They will know that everyone we come across has a huge capacity to hurt us with what we foolishly and unfairly refer to as "small things."

There is likely to be an associated underlying difference in attitudes to money and love in the context of work. For the Frank person, money is the crucial ingredient we want from other people in our professional lives. Therefore they don't feel any great need—in service situations, for example—to express gratitude or take pains to create a semblance of equality with an employee. The waiter or the person at the car-hire desk has, they feel, no special need for kindness on top of the money they will already be getting from the transaction.

Yet the Polite person knows that we take a lot of ourselves into our jobs and need to find respect and a form of love from them as much as we need the cash. So they will be conscious of an additional need to contribute smiles and a pleasant word or two to the person stamping their passport or changing the bedclothes in the hotel. These people are doing their jobs for the money, of course, but payment never invalidates an emotional hunger for a sense of having been useful and appreciated by another person, however brief and functional the encounter may seem.

Grand vs. Small Gestures

The Frank person is often very kind, but in a big way. They are interested in enormous acts of generosity and kindness towards major sections of humanity: perhaps the rescue of the whole continent of Africa or a plan to give every child in the country an equally good start in life. But a consequence of their enthusiasm can be a certain impatience with smaller moves and gestures, which they may view as a distraction from the larger causes. There is no point, they may feel, spending time and money sending people flowers, writing notes after a dinner, or remembering birthdays, when a fundamental transformation of the human condition is at hand.

The Polite person also passionately cares about spreading kindness and love and goodness on a mass scale, but they are cautious about the chances of doing so on any realistic time horizon. Yet their belief that you probably can't improve things for a huge number of people in the coming decades makes them feel that it is still worthwhile trying to make a modest improvement in the lives of the few humans you have direct contact with here and now. They may never be able to transform another person's prospects entirely or rescue our species from its agonies, but they can smile and stop for five minutes to chat to a neighbor about the weather. Their modesty around what is possible makes them acutely sensitive to the worth of the little things that can be done before today is over.

Self-Certainty vs. Self-Doubt

The Frank person has a high degree of confidence in their ability to judge quickly and for the long term what is right and wrong about a given situation. They feel they can tell who has behaved well or badly or what the appropriate course of action should be around a dilemma. This is what gives them the confidence to get angry with what strikes them as rank stupidity, or to blow up bridges with people they've become vexed with, or to state a disagreement emphatically and to call another person stupid, monstrous, or a liar to their face. Once they have said something, they know they can't take it back, but they don't really want to. Part of their frankness is based on the notion that they can understand at speed the merits of any situation, the character of others, and the true nature of their own commitments.

The Polite person is less certain on all these fronts. They are conscious that what they feel strongly about today might not be what they end up thinking next week. They recognize that ideas that sound strange or misguided to them can be attempts to state—in garbled forms—concepts that are genuinely important to other people and that they themselves may come around to with time. They see their own minds as having great capacities for error and as being subject to imperceptible moods that will mislead them—and so are keen not to make statements that can't be taken back or to make enemies of people they might decide are worthy of respect down the line.

The Polite person will be drawn to deploying softening, tentative language and holding back on criticism wherever possible. They will suggest that an idea *might not be quite right*. They will say that a project is *attractive, but that it could be interesting to look at alternatives as well*. They will consider that an intellectual opponent *may well have a point*. They aren't just lying or dodging tough decisions. Their behavior is symptomatic of a nuanced and intelligent belief that few ideas are totally without merit, no proposals are 100 percent wrong, and almost no one is entirely foolish. They work with a conception of the world in which good and bad are deviously entangled and in which bits of the truth are always showing up in unfamiliar guises in unexpected people. Their politeness is a logical, careful response to the complexity they identify in themselves and in the world.

Both the Frank and the Polite person have important lessons to teach us. But it may be that at this point in history, it is the distinctive wisdom of the Polite person that is most ripe for rediscovery and articulation— and that may have the most effective power to take the edge off some of the more brutal and counterproductive consequences of our reigning Frank ideology.

3
Charm

i.
What Is the Purpose of Friendship?

Friendship should be one of the high points of existence, yet it's also the most routinely disappointing reality.

Too often, you're at dinner at someone's house; there's an impressive spread and the hosts have evidently gone to a lot of trouble. But the conversation is meandering and devoid of real interest. It flits from an over-long description of the failings of the inflight service on a particular airline to a strangely heated discussion about the tax code. The intentions of the hosts are hugely touching, but (as so often) we go home wondering what on earth the whole performance was about.

The key to the problem of friendship is found in an odd-sounding place: a lack of a sense of purpose. Our attempts at friendship tend to go adrift, because we collectively resist the task of developing a clear picture of what friendship is really for.

The problem is that we're often uncomfortable with the idea of friendship having any declared purpose, because we associate purpose with the least attractive and most cynical motives. Yet purpose doesn't have to ruin friendship. In fact, the more we define what a friendship is for, the more we can focus on what we should be doing with every person in our lives—or indeed the more we can helpfully conclude that we shouldn't be with someone at all.

There are at least five things we might be trying to do with the people we meet:

1. Networking

Networking is an unfairly maligned idea. We are small, fragile creatures in a vast world. Our individual capacities are insufficient to realize the demands of our imaginations. Therefore, we need collaborators: accomplices who can align their abilities and energies with ours. This idea of friendship was given a lot of space in Classical literature. Take *The Argonauts*, the legendary Ancient Greek tale that traced how a heroic captain called Jason networked in order to assemble a band of friends to sail on the *Argo* in search of the Golden Fleece. Later, the same idea emerged when Jesus networked to put together a band of 12 disciples with whom he could spread one or two world-changing ideas about forgiveness and compassion. Rather than diminish our own efforts as we hand out our business cards, such prestigious examples can show how elevated and ambitious networking friendships could ideally be.

2. Reassurance

The human condition is full of terror. We are always on the verge of disgrace, danger, and disappointment. And yet such are the rules of polite conduct that we are permanently in danger of imagining that we are the only ones to be as crazy as we know we are. We badly need friends because, with the people we know only superficially, there are few confessions of sexual compulsion, regret, rage, and confusion. They refuse to admit that they too are going slightly out of their minds. The reassuring friend gives us access to a very necessary and accurate sense of their own humiliations and follies, an insight with which we can begin to judge ourselves and our sad and compulsive sides more compassionately.

3. Fun

Despite talk of hedonism and immediate gratification, life gives us constant lessons in the need to be serious. We have to guard our dignity, avoid looking like a fool, and pass as a mature adult. The pressure becomes onerous, and in the end even dangerous.

That is why we constantly need access to people we can trust enough to be silly with. They might spend most of their time training to be a neurosurgeon or advising medium-sized companies about their tax liabilities, but when we are together, we can be therapeutically daft. We can put on accents, share lewd fantasies, or doodle on the newspaper, adding a huge nose and a missing front tooth to the president, or giving the fashion model distended ears and masses of curly hair. The fun friend solves the problem of shame around important but unprestigious sides of our selves.

4. Clarifying Our Minds

To a surprising degree, it is very hard to think on our own. The mind is skittish and squeamish. As a result, many issues lie confused within us. We feel angry but are not sure why. Something is wrong with our job but we can't pin it down. The thinking friend holds us to the task. They ask gentle but probing questions that act as a mirror that assists us with the task of knowing ourselves.

5. Holding on to the Past

A number of friends have nothing to say to who we are now, but we keep seeing them, get a little bored in their company—yet are not wrong to retain them in our lives. Perhaps we knew them from school or college, or we once spent a very significant vacation with them 20 years ago, or we became friendly when our children were at kindergarten together. They embody a past version of ourselves from which we're now distant and yet to which we remain loyal. They help us to understand where we have come from and what once mattered. They aren't relevant to who we are today, but not all of our identity is entirely contemporary—as our continued commitment to them attests.

One side effect of seeking more precision about what we're trying to do with our social lives is that we might conclude that, in many cases, we are spending time with people for no truly identifiable reason. These proto-friends share none of our professional ambitions or interests; they aren't reassuring and may in fact be secretly excited by the possibility of our failure; we can't be cathartically silly around them; they aren't interested in furthering either our or their path to self-knowledge and they aren't connected with important phases of our lives.

They are simply in our orbit as a result of an unhappy accident that we have been too sentimental to correct.

We should dare to be a little ruthless. Culling acquaintances isn't a sign that we have lost belief in friendship. It is evidence that we are becoming clearer and more demanding about what a friendship could be. In the best way, the price of knowing what friendship is for may be a few more evenings in our own company.

ii.
The Problem of Over-Friendliness

There is a particularly poignant way to be a social disaster: through over-friendliness, a pattern of behavior driven by the very best of motives that ends up feeling as irritating as outright rudeness.

We meet the over-friendly at the office, laughing at the jokes of the senior management; behind the desk at the hotel, wishing Sir or Madam a highly enjoyable stay; and across the table on a first date, lavishly endorsing their would-be partner's every opinion about recent books and movies.

The over-friendly are guilty of three large errors:

–   First, they believe they must agree on everything. If the other says the world is going to the dogs, they immediately nod in consent. If, a second later, there is a prediction of a utopian technological future, they will agree just as much. When we say something clever, they are thrilled. When we say something daft, they like it no less. Their ritual approval may seem attentive. In truth, it's a version of not listening at all.

–   Second, their praise is ill-targeted. Plenty of nice things are being said, but they are not the ones we happen to value. They claim to love our umbrella, our credit card is from their favorite bank, our chairs are deeply beautiful, we apparently have a nice way of holding our fork ... but none of this counts for us if it isn't connected up with our own sense of meaning and achievement. Everyone loves being praised, but to be praised inaccurately is its own kind of insult.

–   Third, their friendliness is remorselessly upbeat. They point out how well we look, how impressive our job sounds, how perfect our family life seems. They want to make us feel good, but they dangerously raise the cost of revealing any of the lonelier, darker, more melancholic aspects of our characters.

By contrast, the less ardently friendly and therefore properly pleasing person will keep three things closely in mind:

–   First, that disagreement isn't necessarily terrible—it may be exhilarating to be contradicted when we don't feel that our dignity is at stake and we are learning something valuable at the hands of a combative interlocutor.

–   Second, that people only want to be complimented on things they are actively proud of. The value of the currency of praise depends on it not being spent too freely. The truly pleasing person knows they must pass over many things in discreet silence; when they eventually do bestow a blessing, their words have a proper resonance.

– Third, that we are cheered up not so much by people who say cheery things as by people who appear to understand us. This usually means people who sympathize with our sorrows and show a willingness to travel with us to the anxious, hesitant, or confused parts of our psyches.

What enables the pleasing person to please is their capacity to hold on in social encounters, even with rather intimidating and alien-seeming people, to an intimate knowledge of what satisfies them. They instinctively use their own experience as a base for thinking about the needs of others. By contrast, the over-friendly person allows themselves to forget their own likes and dislikes, under the pressure of an excessive humility that suggests to them that anyone impressive could not possibly share in the principles that drive their own psychology.

At the core of the pleasing person's charm is a metaphysical insight: that other people cannot, deep down, be very "other." Therefore, in core ways, what one knows about oneself will be the master key to understanding and getting along with strangers—not in every case, but enough of the time to make the difference.

Over-friendliness is not just a feature of one-to-one encounters; it is an entrenched flaw within modern consumer society more generally. This explains why the airline exuberantly wishes us a perfect day upon landing in a new city; why the waiter hopes we'll have a truly wonderful time eating the first course; and why the attendant in a clothing store pulls such a large smile along with their suggestion that we try on a new pair of pants.

Here, too, the cause of an asphyxiating friendliness is a sudden modesty and loss of confidence around using oneself as a guide to the temperament and needs of a stranger. Companies become over-impressed by the apparent "otherness" of their clients and thereby overlook how many aspects of their own selves are being trampled upon in a service context. They sidestep the knowledge that just after landing back home after a trip abroad, we may feel horrified at the thought of our responsibilities in the family; or that moods of introversion and sadness can accompany us even inside a clothes boutique. They behave as if they were cheerful Martians encountering broken, complex humans for the very first time.

The fault of the excessively over-friendly person can often be traced back to a touching modesty. They are guilty of nothing more than a loss of confidence in the validity of their own experiences as a guide to the pleasure of others. The failure of the over-friendly types teaches us that in order to succeed at pleasing anyone, we must first accept the risk that we might displease them through a candid expression of our being. Successful charm relies on an initial secure sense that we could survive social failure. Rehearsing how it would in the end be OK to make a hash of seducing someone is perhaps the best way to seduce them properly and confidently. We must reconcile ourselves to the risk of not making friends to stand any chance of actually making any.

iii.
How to Overcome Shyness

Because shyness can grip us in such powerful ways, it is tempting to think of it as an immutable part of our emotional makeup, with roots that extend far into our personality and perhaps biology that we could never extirpate. But in truth, shyness is based on a set of ideas about the world that are eminently amenable to change through a process of reason because they are founded on some touchingly malleable errors of thought.

Shyness is rooted in a distinctive way of interpreting strangers. The shy aren't awkward around everyone; they are tongue-tied around those who seem most unlike them on the basis of a range of surface markers: of age, class, tastes, habits, beliefs, backgrounds, or religions. With no unkindness meant, we could define shyness as a form of "provincialism" of the mind, an overattachment to the incidentals of one's own life and experience that unfairly casts others into the role of daunting, unfathomable, unknowable foreigners.

On contact with a person from another world or "province," the shy allow their minds to be dominated by a forbidding aura of difference. They may (silently and awkwardly) say to themselves that there is nothing to be done or said because the other is famous while they belong to the province of the obscure; or because the other is very old while their province is that of 20-somethings; or because the other is very clever while their province is that of the nonintellectual; or because the other is from the land of very beautiful girls while they hail from the province of average-looking boys. This is why there can be no grounds to laugh, to hazard a playful remark, or to feel at ease. The shy person doesn't intend to be unpleasant or unfriendly. They simply experience all otherness as an insurmountable barrier to making their own goodwill and personality apparent.

We can imagine that, in the history of humanity, shyness was always the first response. The people over the hill would have triggered the feeling because they were farmers while you were fishermen, or they spoke with a lilt in their vowels while your diction was monotone and flat.

Yet, gradually there emerged a more worldly, less exclusive, way of relating to strangers: what we might call a psychological "cosmopolitanism." In the ancient civilizations of Greece and Rome, prompted by ever-increasing encounters between peoples who lived very different and mutually unfamiliar lives, thanks to developments in trade and shipping, an alternative to shyness developed. Greek travelers who worshipped humanlike divinities learned that Egyptians revered cats and certain birds. Romans who shaved their chins met barbarians who did not. Senators who lived in colonnaded houses with underfloor heating encountered chieftains who lived in drafty wooden huts. Among certain thinkers, an approach developed that proposed that all these humans, whatever their surface variations, shared a common core—and that it was to this that the mature mind should turn in contact with apparent otherness. It was to this "cosmopolitan" mindset that the Roman playwright and poet Terence gave voice when he wrote: "I am human: nothing human is foreign to me," and that Christianity made use of in rendering universal sympathy a cornerstone of its view of existence.

Someone becomes a cosmopolitan not on the basis of having a buoyant or gregarious nature but because they are in touch with a fundamental truth about humanity, because they know that, irrespective of appearance, we are the same species beneath, an insight that the tongue-tied guest at the party or the awkward seducer in the restaurant are guilty of implicitly refusing.

The cosmopolitan is well aware of differences between people. They just refuse to be cowed or dominated by them. They look beyond them to perceive, or in practical terms simply to guess at, a collective species unity. The stranger may not know your friends from elementary school, may not have read the same novels or have met your parents, may wear a dress, or a large hat and beard or be in their eighth decade or only a few days past being 4 years old, but the cosmopolitan won't be daunted by the lack of local points of reference. They are sure they will stumble somewhere upon common ground—even if it takes a couple of false starts. All human beings (however varied their outward appearance) must—they know—be activated by a few basic dimensions of concern. There will be uniting likes, hates, hopes, and fears, even if it is only a love of rolling a ball back and forth or a mutual interest in sunbathing.

The shy provincial is a pessimist at heart. The modernizer won't—they feel certain—be able to talk to the traditionalist; the enthusiast of the left must have no time for anyone on the right; the atheist won't be able to engage with the priest; the business owner must get awkward around the socialist. The confident cosmopolitan, by contrast, starts from the assumption that people are endowed with wildly opposed views, but that these need never fatally undermine the rich range of similarities that will remain in other areas.

Traditionally, rank or status has been a major source of shy provincialism: The peasant felt he could not approach the lord; the young milkmaid stammered when the earl's son visited the stable. Today, in an echo of such inhibitions, the person of average looks feels they could never hang out with the very beautiful woman, or the modestly off imagine they can't talk to the very wealthy. The mind fixates on the gulf: My nose looks as if a child had modeled it out of plasticine, yours as if Michelangelo had carved it; I fear losing my job, while you fear that expanding your business into Germany won't be as profitable as you'd forecast.

Shyness has its insightful dimensions. It is infused with an awareness that we might be bothering someone with our presence; it is based on an acute sense that a stranger could be dissatisfied or discomfited by us. The shy person is touchingly alive to the dangers of being a nuisance. Someone with no capacity for shyness is a scary possibility, for they operate with a dismaying attitude of entitlement. They are so composed and sure only because they haven't taken on board the possibility that another person might rightly have a disenchanted view of them.

In most cases, we pay an unnecessarily heavy price for our reserve around people who might open their hearts to us, if only we knew how to manifest our own benevolence. We cling too jealously to our province. The pimply boy doesn't discover that he and the high-school beauty share a taste in humor and similarly painful relationships with their fathers; the middle-aged lawyer never unearths a shared love of rockets with her neighbor's 8-year-old son. Races and ages continue not to mingle, to their collective detriments. Shyness is a touching, yet ultimately excessive and unwarranted, way of feeling special.

iv.
Why Affectionate Teasing Is Kind and Necessary

It may not seem like it, but teasing done with affection and skill is a profound human accomplishment.

There's nasty teasing, of course, in which we pick at a sore spot in someone's life. But we're talking here of the affectionate version, something generous and loving, which feels good to be on the receiving end of.

It may be lovely to be teased when, for example, you're a teenager and in a grumpy, sullen mood, and your kindly dad nicknames you Hamlet, after Shakespeare's Danish prince of gloom. Or when you're 45 and pretty serious in business and your old college friends call you by the name they made up for you aged 19, the night you failed dismally in trying to pick up a German student who was in town.

All of us become a bit unbalanced in one way or another: too serious, too gloomy, too jokey. We all benefit from being tugged back towards a healthier mean. The good teaser latches onto and responds to our distinctive imbalances and is compassionately constructive about trying to change us: Not by delivering a stern lesson, but by helping us to notice our excesses and to laugh at them. We sense the teaser is trying to give us a useful shove in a good (and secretly welcome) direction and therefore know that, at its affectionate best, teasing is both sweet and constructive.

The English literary critic Cyril Connolly once famously wrote: "Imprisoned in every fat man a thin man is wildly signalling to be let out."

This is a general idea with multiple variants: Inside the fussy, over-formal individual there's a more relaxed person looking for an opening; there's an ambitious, eager self quietly despairing within the lazy man; the gloomy, disenchanted cynic harbors a more cheery, sunny subself in need of more recognition.

The teasing remark speaks over the head of the dominant aspect to the subordinated side of the self, whom it helps to release and relax.

There's a moment in *The Line of Beauty*—a novel by Alan Hollinghurst, set in the 1980s—in which Nick, the charming young central character, is invited to a grand party and meets the British prime minister, Margaret Thatcher. Everyone else is slightly terrified of her, but Nick warmly and teasingly suggests that she might like to dance to a pop song. The other guests are horrified— she's meant to be obsessed by stringent economic reform and hard-nosed politics—but, after a brief inner struggle, she replies with a smile: "You know, I'd like that very much." (Perhaps if, in reality, there had been more people to tease her, the pop-loving, dancing side of Mrs Thatcher might have played a greater role in national affairs—and history would have been different.)

When we enjoy being warmly teased, it's because the teasing remark emerges from a genuine insight into who we are. This person has studied us and put their finger on a struggle that's going on in us; they've taken the part of a nice—but currently under-supported—side of who we are. It's pleasing because normally others don't see much past the front we put on for the world. Typically, the world just thinks we are gloomy, or stern, or intellectual, or obsessed by fashion. The teaser does us the favor of recognizing that the dominant front isn't telling the whole story; they're kind enough and perceptive enough to see past the surface.

Perhaps the most instructive question we can ask— the one that teaches us most about the value of affectionate teasing—is simply: What do I need to be teased about?

V.
How to Be Warm

While politeness is of course always preferable to rudeness, there are ways of being polite that badly miss the mark and can leave us feeling oddly detached and dissatisfied. Picture the person who ends up, despite their best efforts, seeming what we can call coldly polite. They may be keen to please those they are seeing, they obey all the rules of etiquette, offer their guests drinks, ask them questions about their journey, suggest they might want a little more gravy, remark on the interest of a recent prizewinning novel—yet never manage to make their hospitality feel either engaging or memorable. It may be a long time before another meeting with them is suggested.

By contrast, there is the person we recognize as warm, who follows the cold person in the basic principles of politeness, but manages to add a critical emotionally comforting ingredient to their manner. They might, when we have an evening planned with them, suggest making grilled cheese sandwiches at their place rather than going out to a restaurant; they might chat to us through the bathroom door; put on the songs they loved dancing to when they were 14; plump up a cushion and slot it behind our back; confess to feeling intimidated by a mutual acquaintance; bring us a posy of daisies or a card they made; call us when we're sick with the flu and ask how our ears are feeling; make encouraging "mmm" and "ah" sounds to show sympathy and interest for a story they've teased out of us about our insomnia; give us a sly conspiratorial wink when they notice we're finding someone else at the table attractive; mention they like our haircut, and then, when we spill something or fart by mistake, exclaim: "I'm so glad you did that! Usually it's me."

Beneath the difference between the warm and the cold person lies a contrasting vision of human nature. Broadly, the cold person is operating with an implicit view that those they are attempting to please are creatures endowed only with the highest needs. As a result, all kinds of assumptions are made about them: that they are interested exclusively in so-called serious topics (especially art and politics); that they will appreciate a degree of formality in dining and sitting; that they will be strong, self-contained, and mature enough not to have any hunger for reassurance or coziness; and that they will be without urgent physical vulnerabilities and drives, which might prove deeply offensive if they were mentioned. These higher beings would, the cold host believes, wince if someone suggested they curl up on the couch with a blanket or handed them a copy of a magazine about movie stars when they headed for the bathroom.

Yet, the warmly polite person is always deeply aware that the stranger is (irrespective of their status or outward

Charm

dignity) a highly needy, fragile, confused, appetitive, and susceptible creature. They know this about the stranger because they never forget this about themselves. Warmly polite people have much in common with the character Kanga, the tenderly maternal kangaroo in A.A. Milne's Winnie-the-Pooh books. In one of the stories, the animals are disconcerted by the arrival in the Hundred Acre Wood of Tigger, who is very big, very loud, and bouncy and assertive. They treat him with caution and are—we might say—coldly polite. But when Tigger finally meets Kanga, she is immediately warm with him. She thinks of him in much the same terms as she does her own child, Roo: "Just because an animal is large, it doesn't mean he doesn't want kindness; however big Tigger seems to be, remember that he wants as much kindness as Roo," says Kanga, in what might be a definition of the philosophy of warmth.

Sometimes it is deeply generous to think that another person may be more elevated than us. Collectively we've taken this thought very much to heart. We have internalized distance and learned caution, moving on from the naivety of the small child who wonders sweetly when you are sad whether you might like to sniff their grimy blanket.

This has given rise to a touchingly sad possibility that the other is much more involved in our kind of vulnerabilities than they let on or that we dare to suppose.

85

Two people may be secretly yearning for the same modest thing while each being too polite (that is, too under the sway of a cold interpretation of human nature) to properly recognize or act upon their desires.

The warmly polite person may not hold to an explicit theory of what they are doing, but at root their conduct is based on an understanding that however solid and dignified someone appears on the outside, behind the scenes there will inevitably be a struggling self, potentially awkward, easily bemused, beset by physical appetites, on the verge of loneliness—and frequently in need of nothing more subtle or elevated than a cheese sandwich, a glass of milk, and a hug.

vi.
Why Flirting Matters

Flirting has a bad name. Too often, it seems a form of duplicity, a sly attempt to excite another person and derive gratification from their interest without any corresponding wish to go to bed with them. It looks like a manipulative promise of sexual affection that, at the last moment, leaves its targets confused and humiliated. In our sadness, back home alone after the nightclub or the party, we may rail against the flirt for "only" flirting, when it had appeared there might be so much more.

But this pattern represents only one, unedifying and regrettable, possibility around flirting. At its best, flirting can be a vital social process that generously lends us reassurance and freely redistributes confidence and self-esteem. The task is not to stop flirting, but to learn how better to practice its most honorable versions.

Good flirting is in essence an attempt, driven by kindness and imaginative excitement, to inspire another person to believe more firmly in their own likability— psychological as much as physical. It is a gift offered not in order to manipulate, but out of a pleasure at perceiving what is most attractive in another. Along the way, the good flirt must carefully convince us of three apparently contradictory things: that they would love to sleep with us; that they won't sleep with us; and that the reason why has nothing to do with any deficiency on our part.

Good flirting exploits—with no evil intent—an important truth about sex: that what is often most enjoyable about sex is not the physical process itself so much as the idea of acceptance that underpins the act; the notion that another person likes us enough to accept us in our most raw and vulnerable state and is, in turn, willing to lose control and surrender aspects of their own everyday dignity. It is this concept, far more than the deft touching of skin, that contributes the dominant share of our pleasure as we undress someone for the first time or heed their request to call them the rudest words we know.

The good flirt knows this and is therefore spared a guilty sense that they might not be in a position to offer their lovers anything valuable. They are wisely convinced that it is eminently possible, simply over a dinner table or in the kitchen at work, to gift a person just about the most wondrous aspect of sex itself—simply through the medium of language.

The good flirt is an expert too in how correctly to frame the fact that there won't be sex. By a deeply entrenched quirk of the human mind, it is generally hard for us to hear such news without reaching one overwhelming and crushing conclusion: that the seducer has suddenly found us deeply and pervasively repulsive. The good flirt loosens us from such punitive narratives. They powerfully appeal to some of the many genuine reasons why two people might not have sex that have nothing to do with one person finding the other disgusting: for example, because one or both of them already has a partner, because there is an excessive age gap, a gender incompatibility, an office that would disapprove, a difficult family situation, or, most simply, a lack of time.

Freed from the rigid and blunt supposition that flirting has to be a prelude to actual sex, the good flirt can artfully imply how different things might have been if the world had been more ideally arranged. The recipient of the flirt can, with equal grace, assent to the story without a need to twist it through self-hatred.

We all need reminders of what is tolerable and exciting about us. It is a desperate foreshortening of possibilities to insist that such reawakening can only be justified by actual intercourse. Understood properly, flirting can beneficially occur across the largest gulfs: gulfs of political belief, of social, economic, or marital status, of sexual inclination and (with obvious caveats) of age. The 26-year-old corporate lawyer and the 52-year-old behind the counter of the grocery store can flirt; and so may the cleaner and the CEO. It is all the more moving when they do so because it signals a willingness to use the imagination to locate what is most attractive about another person who lies very far from one's own area of familiarity. The question of what, if I considered someone, anyone, sexually, I would find charming is one of the most intimate, interesting, and necessary questions one can ask.

The good flirt needs skill to home in on the less obvious, but still very real, ways in which everyone can be attractive. They might draw attention to a nicely shaped elbow or to a characteristic intelligent tilt of the head. They must actively search for the location of another person's sexual allure, piecing together a portrait like a great novelist gradually revealing the hidden charm of an apparently ordinary character. Like Jesus, they are giving attention to the secret goodness of someone who (to the hasty glance of others) will appear an outcast or a sinner unworthy of love.

We have for too long been warned against flirting by an unfortunate Romantic ideal of total coherence, one that implies that either we are completely sincere in flirting and so must make love or we are, in effect, liars. In many Romantic novels of the 19th century, "flirt" is, therefore, a term of abuse. No hero or heroine could ever adopt a playful, semierotic tone with anyone except their true love. But they would thereby miss out on an important enlargement of their sensibilities.

The ideal flirtation is a small work of social art cocreated by two people, a civilized artifice that acknowledges limitations, worries about consequences, and knows the importance of not letting momentary impulses damage long-standing commitments. It knows that avoiding sex is usually wise, but is intelligently invested in sharing some of the benefits of sex without the act itself.

The good flirt isn't making things up; they are not merely flattering or manipulating. They are offering us a view we very rarely get of ourselves as desirable. A few people, of course, have an excessive belief in their own attractiveness. But mostly we suffer gravely in the opposite direction. We generally learn—through a rich sequence of rebuffs and criticisms and via intelligent modesty that alerts us to our own shortcomings—to see ourselves as far from ideal. We know we're in some ways not terribly lovable or exceptionally alluring. This picture of ourselves is not inaccurate but is not entirely true either.

The good flirt carries out an important psychological mission: to restore balance to our view of ourselves. They remind us that, for all our failings of character and bodily liabilities, we are, in certain ways, properly appealing and, in a better situation than the one we find ourselves in, a truly interesting person to want to spend a night with. The flirt supplies an antidote to a characteristic sickness of maturity: an excessively negative view of ourselves. It is because we are so prone to self-hatred, so liable to forget how to appreciate ourselves properly, that we need more vigorously, and with fewer qualms, to engage in the important business of flirting with one another.

The good flirt is doing crucially important social

work, via a well-timed smirk, a coyly arched eyebrow, a quiet observation, or an expectedly warm remark. They understand that being recognized as erotically appealing is a hugely beneficial and ethical need of the soul, because feeling desirable is key to rendering us more patient, more generous, more energetic, and more content. It is a quiet tragedy that this widely consequential need should so often be expected to pass through the desperately narrow gate of sex.

The good flirt wisely and liberally rebels against such a stricture. Their mission is to give erotic endorsement (and all the benefits this brings) a larger opportunity in life, liberating it from the tiny, difficult window of opportunity offered by an actual requirement to start to make love. The flirt knows how to broaden the circle of attractiveness. They know—in essence—how to love someone without needing to give more than they should ever realistically be expected to. The ideal flirt is a pioneer in a crucial democratic science: They are attempting to correctly identify attractiveness in a way that will serve the many rather than the few. We should not only be grateful to good flirts; we should try to become good flirts ourselves.

vii.
Why Kind People Always Lie

Truly good people are always ready and even, at times, highly enthusiastic about telling lies. This sounds odd only because we are in the grip of a heroic but indiscriminate and delusional addiction to truth telling.

A lot of this can be blamed on the first president of the United States, George Washington. Legend recounts how, at the age of 6, he was given a little ax as a present. He was so excited with the gift that he went straight into the garden and hacked down a beautiful cherry tree. His father was furious when he discovered the tree and asked George if he was responsible. The boy was said to have replied: "Father, I cannot tell a lie. It was I." The story is probably apocryphal, but it has stuck because it encapsulates an ideal to which we are intensely collectively committed: a devotion to the truth in spite of the cost it exacts on oneself. In this scenario, the liar is odious because they seek to evade a necessary and important truth for the sake of low personal gain.

But good people do not lie for their own benefit. They aren't protecting themselves and they aren't disloyal to the facts out of mendacity: They tell lies because (paradoxical as it sounds at first) they love the truth intensely—and out of good will for the person they are deceiving.

We are ready enough to admit to a role for lies in

certain situations. You might be visiting an elderly aunt who prides herself on her talent for carrot cakes with vanilla frosting. But her heyday is long gone. Now she muddles up the recipe and sometimes forgets how long the butter has been in the refrigerator. The result is pretty off-putting. But it's deeply important for her to feel that she's still able to please others. That's why you lie.

The lie isn't produced to protect oneself. It is told out of loyalty to a bigger truth—that one loves the aunt—that would be threatened by full disclosure. As is so often the case, a great truth has to pass into the mind of another person via a smaller falsehood.

What makes falsehoods so necessary is our proclivity for making unfortunate associations. It is, of course, entirely possible to love someone deeply and at the same time believe they are terrible at baking. But in our own minds, the rejection of our cakes tends to feel synonymous with the rejection of our being. We're forcing any half-decent person to lie to us by the obtuseness of our thought processes. It is because the aunt is in the grip of a falsehood ("If you don't like my cake, you can't like me") that we will have to offer her a dose of untruth ("I like your cake") by which we can make sure that a bigger truth ("I like you") remains safe.

The same principle applies in more tricky situations. Suppose a woman goes away to a conference. One night, after a lovely conversation in the bar, she gets carried away and slips into bed with an international colleague. They don't make love but have a sweet time. They rub their lips together and entwine their legs. They will almost certainly never see one another again; it wasn't an attempt to start a long-term relationship, and it meant very little. When the woman gets home, her partner asks how her evening was. She says she watched CNN and ordered a club sandwich in her room on her own.

She lies because she knows her partner well and can predict how he would respond to the truth. He would be wounded to the core, would be convinced that his wife didn't love him and would probably conclude that divorce was the only option.

But this assessment of the truth would not be accurate. In reality, it is entirely possible to love someone deeply but go to bed with another person every so often. And yet, kind people understand the entrenched and socially endorsed associations between infidelity and callousness. For almost all of us, the news "I spent a night with a colleague from the Singapore office" (which is true) has to end up meaning "I don't love you anymore" (which is not true). So we have to say "I didn't sleep with anyone" (which is untrue) in the name of securing the greater idea: "I still love you" (which is overwhelmingly true).

However much they love the truth, good people have an even greater commitment to something else:

being kind towards others. They grasp (and make allowances for) the ease with which a truth can produce unhelpful convictions in the minds of others and are therefore not overcommitted to accuracy at every turn. Their loyalty is reserved for something they take to be far more important than literal narration: the sanity and well-being of their audiences. Telling the truth, they understand, isn't a matter of the sentence-by-sentence veracity of one's words; it's a matter of ensuring that, after one has spoken, the other person can be left with an accurate picture of reality.

This concern for the well-being of others explains why kind people only ever lie when there is little chance of their untruths being detected. They know that a lie that gets unearthed will cause proper and unjustifiable trouble, leading the other person to a second and even more radically false conclusion: Not only that "you don't love me" (first untruth) but also that "you lied to me because you don't love me" (a second, even greater, untruth).

It can feel condescending to hear the logic of the good liar spelled out. But that's only because we don't like to acknowledge the fragility of our own minds. We may believe we are heroically ready to embrace the truth, however painful. We may insist that others should tell us everything, whatever they do. But we thereby discount our own powerful tendencies to emotional indigestion. It's why we should not only occasionally tell untruths, but actively hope that, from time to time, others will lie to us—and quietly hope that we will never find out that they have.

viii.
How to Be a Good Listener

Being a good listener is one of the most important and enchanting life skills anyone can have. Yet few of us know how to do it; not because we are evil, but because no one has taught us how, and—on a related point—few have listened sufficiently well to us. So we come to social life greedy to speak rather than listen, hungry to meet others, but reluctant to hear them. Friendship degenerates into a socialized egoism.

As with most things, the answer lies in education. Our civilization is full of useful books on how to speak— Cicero's *Orator* and Aristotle's *Rhetoric* were two of the greatest from the ancient world—but sadly no one has ever written a book called *The Listener*. There is a range of things that the good listener is doing that makes it so pleasant to spend time in their company.

Without necessarily realizing it, we are often propelled into conversation by something that feels both urgent and somehow undefined. We're bothered at work; we're toying with more ambitious career moves; we're not sure if so and so is right for us; a relationship is in difficulties; we're fretting about something or feeling a bit low about life in general (without being able to put a finger on exactly what's wrong); or perhaps we're very excited and enthusiastic about something—though the reasons for our passion are tricky to pin down.

At heart, all these are issues in search of elucidation. The good listener knows that we'd ideally move—via conversation with another person—from a confused and agitated state of mind to one that was more focused and serene. Together, we would work out what was really at stake. But, in reality, this tends not to happen because there isn't enough awareness of the desire for clarification within conversation; there aren't enough good listeners. People tend to assert rather than analyze. They restate in many different ways the fact that they are worried, excited, sad, or hopeful. And their interlocutor listens, but doesn't assist them to discover more.

Good listeners fight against this with a range of conversational gambits. They hover as the other speaks; they offer remarks of support; they make gentle, positive gestures: a sigh of sympathy, a nod of encouragement, a strategic "hmm" of interest. All the time they are egging the other to go deeper into issues. They love saying: "tell me more about …"; "I was fascinated when you said …"; "why did that happen, do you think?", or "how did you feel about that?"

The good listener takes it for granted that they will encounter vagueness in the conversation of others. But they don't condemn, rush, or become impatient, because they see vagueness as a universal and highly significant trouble of the mind that it is the task of a true friend to

help with. The good listener never forgets how hard—
and how important—it is to know our own minds. Often,
we're in the vicinity of something, but we can't quite close
in on what's really bothering or exciting us. The good
listener knows we benefit hugely from encouragement to
elaborate, to go into greater detail, to push a little further.
We need someone who, rather than launch forth, will
simply say two rare magic words: "Go on ..."

You mention a sibling and they want to know a bit
more. What was the relationship like in childhood? How
has it changed over time? They are curious where our
concerns and excitements come from. They ask things
like: Why did that particularly bother you? Why was that
such a big thing for you? They keep our histories in mind,
they might refer back to something we said before and
we feel they're building up a deeper base of engagement.

It is fatally easy to say vague things: We might
mention that something is lovely or terrible, nice or
annoying. But we don't really explore why we feel
this way. The good listener has a productive, friendly
suspicion of some of our own first statements and is after
the deeper attitudes that are lurking in the background.
They take things we say like "I'm fed up with my job" or
"My partner and I are having a lot of rows ..." and help
us to concentrate on what it really is about the job we
don't like or what the rows might be about deep down.

They're bringing to listening an ambition to clear

up underlying issues. They don't just see conversation as the swapping of anecdotes. They are reconnecting the chat you're having over pizza with the philosophical ambitions of Socrates, whose dialogues were records of his attempts to help his fellow Athenians understand and examine their own underlying ideas and values.

A key move of the good listener is not always to follow every byway or subplot that the speaker introduces, for they may be getting lost and further from their own point than they would themselves wish. The good listener is helpfully suspicious, knowing that their purpose is to focus the fundamental themes of the speaker, rather than veering off with them into every side road. They are always looking to take the speaker back to their last reasonable point—saying, "Yes, yes, but you were saying just a moment ago ...". Or, "So, ultimately, what do you think it was about ...?" The good listener (paradoxically) is a skilled interrupter. But they don't (as most people do) interrupt to intrude their own ideas; they interrupt to help the other person get back to their original, more sincere, yet elusive concerns.

The good listener doesn't moralize. They know their own minds well enough not to be surprised or frightened by strangeness. They know how insane we all are. That's why others can feel comfortable being heard by them. They give the impression they recognize and accept our follies; they don't flinch when we mention a particular desire. They reassure us they're not going to shred our dignity. A big worry in a competitive world is that we feel we can't afford to be honest about how distressed or obsessed we are. Saying one feels like a failure or a pervert could mean being dropped.

The good listener signals early and clearly that they don't see us in these terms. Our vulnerability is something they warm to rather than are appalled by. It is only too easy to end up experiencing ourselves as strangely cursed and exceptionally deviant or uniquely incapable. But the good listener makes their own strategic confessions, so as to set the record straight about the meaning of being a normal human being—that is, very muddled and radically imperfect. They confess not so much to unburden themselves as to help others accept their own nature and see that being a bad parent, a poor lover, or a confused worker are not malignant acts of wickedness, but ordinary features of being alive that others have unfairly edited out of their public profiles.

When we are in the company of people who listen well, we experience a very powerful pleasure, but too often we don't realize what this person is doing that is so nice. By paying strategic attention to our feelings of satisfaction, we can learn to magnify them and offer them to others, who will notice, heal—and repay the favor in turn. Listening deserves discovery as one of the keys to a good society.

ix.
How to Be Open-Minded

One of the distinctive features of social life is that most of the people we meet seem quite normal. They often appear reasonably responsible and logical, harbor little self-hatred or compulsion and strike us as cheerful and more or less content with their partners and their lives.

This can feel hugely and horribly at odds with what we know of life from our own minds. Beyond a certain age, once we have lived a little inside ourselves, we tend to become acquainted with a range of deeply alarming and regrettable sides to our characters: We recognize the extent of our confusion, compulsion, sexual waywardness, disloyalty, meanness, insecurity, and peculiarity.

This gap between the knowledge we have of ourselves and the public evidence of the nature of others can end up feeling intensely bewildering and painful. We may wonder why we may have ended up quite so strange, our lives so difficult, our characters so crooked.

Our sense of isolation is never greater than when we run into the armies, widely distributed through society, of the closed-minded. Full of broadly benevolent intention, these types nevertheless keep a close eye on any signs of the more regrettable aspects of human nature and are ready to censor their appearance from the first. We learn to recognize their disapproval and to keep our shadow sides especially private in their vicinity—which protects our reputations but increases our underlying sense of freakish isolation.

By contrast, there are those rare individuals who seem able to take most of what we are for granted from the first—and whom we gratefully honor with the term "open-minded." Without particular surprise or fuss, they assume from the first that being human is a messy and impure business and that any person they come across is likely to contain a host of less than ideal dimensions and at points be really quite close to madness. They know, simply on the basis of your membership of the human race, that you have thought and done a range of wild, unethical, and sometimes lamentable things. They don't know the details, but they correctly assume the broad shape of the issue. They calmly accept the gap between how a person appears and what they are probably like in private. For them, a person who seems normal is just someone they don't yet know very well.

The open-minded are unafraid of what is inside the human soul for two reasons: first, because they are confident that there is in almost everyone a huge and secure gap between feelings and actions. They understand that most of what we fantasize about will never be played out in reality and therefore doesn't pose an active threat either to ourselves or to the social order. We may spend a lot of time entertaining what we'll say to our enemies, how we'll give up on everything and everyone (and the world will be sorry), and crafting lurid sexual scenarios contrary to every civilized dictate. But, as the open-minded know, fantasizing is not a prelude to action: it's an alternative to it. So our odder'thoughts can be looked at, discussed, and sometimes laughed over—in the secure knowledge that they will eventually be put back safely in the box. What's more, such examination won't aggravate them; it will help to contain and neuter them.

The open-minded also know that the existence of highly troublesome elements doesn't preclude the simultaneous presence of vast zones of goodness, humility, and benevolence in our characters. They are implicitly fond of the distinction, formulated by early Christian thinkers, between "the sinner" and "the sin." Like St Augustine, they strive to "love the sinner but hate the sin." They know that our right to charity, attention, and friendship should not be irrevocably lost on the basis of our darker sides. While hoping it might be otherwise, the open-minded simply take it for granted that nice people constantly do and think not very nice things.

The open-minded person isn't merely being sweet in calmly accepting this as a given, and therefore not judging harshly when news of misdeeds arises. They are committed to open-mindedness because they are operating with a picture of how people can improve. They implicitly propose that the way we change is through warm forgiveness, not cold censure.

The closed-minded are also committed to improvement, but their philosophy of education involves humiliation and disapproval. Only if a person can be brought to hate themselves enough, they reason, can they be counted upon to start to want to change their ways.

The problem is not only that this fostering of self-contempt can be very cruel; it is also liable to be ineffective. Self-contempt tends to badly sap the will and renders us hopeless and incapable before its ravages. In the face of it, we may seek refuge in our vices to escape our violent dislike of ourselves and of our less admirable characteristics. By the angle of their lips and their moments of silence, the closed-minded act as proactive agents of a counterproductive loneliness. They create a world in which significant parts of ourselves must remain homeless and without a path to redemption.

The open-minded know that most people are already brim-full of self-criticism. We're not in need of further, harder condemnation. Where we truly need help is in liking ourselves enough to dare to develop, given what we know of the sinister regions of our psyches. By their unshocked reception of the stranger elements of who we are, combined with supportive exhortations to betterment, the open-minded model for us the relationship we would ideally have with ourselves as we strive to encourage the nobler parts of our nature and overcome the weakest. It is easy to see why we should so badly want them as friends.

x.
How Not to Be Boring

One of our great fears—which haunts us when we go into the world and socialize with others—is that we may be boring.

But the good news, and a fundamental truth too, is that no one is *ever truly* boring. They are only in danger of coming across as such when they either fail to understand their deeper selves or don't dare (or know how) to communicate them to others.

That there is simply no such thing as an inherently boring person or thing is one of the great lessons of art. Many of the most satisfying art works don't feature exalted or rare elements; they are about the ordinary looked at in a special way, with unusual sincerity and openness to unvarnished experience. Take, for example, some grasses painted by the Danish artist Christen Købke in a suburb of Copenhagen in 1837. Outwardly, the scene is unremarkable and could initially appear to be unpromising material for a painting, and yet—like any great artist—Købke knew how to interrogate his own perceptions in a fresh, unclouded, underivative manner and translate them accurately into his medium, weaving a small masterpiece out of the thread of everyday life.

Just as there is no such thing as a boring riverbank, tree, or dandelion, so too there can be no such thing as an

Christen Købke, *View of Dosseringen, Copenhagen, with Willows in the Foreground*, c. 1837. Købke elevates what at first looks like an unremarkable piece of landscape into a beautiful artwork through close attention.

inherently boring person. The human animal witnessed in its essence, with honesty and without artifice, is always interesting. When we call a person boring, we are just pointing to someone who has not had the courage or concentration to tell us what it is like to be them. By contrast, we invariably prove compelling when we succeed in saying how and what we truly desire, envy, regret, mourn, and dream. Anyone who faithfully captures the real data on what it is like to exist is guaranteed to have material with which to captivate others. The interesting person isn't someone to whom obviously and outwardly interesting things have happened—someone who has traveled the world, met important dignitaries, or been present at large geopolitical events. Nor is it someone who speaks in learned terms about the weighty themes of culture, history, or science. They are someone who has grown into an attentive, self-aware listener, and a reliably honest correspondent of the tremors of their own mind and heart, and who can thereby give us faithful accounts of the pathos, drama, and strangeness of being alive.

What, then, are some of the elements that get in the way of us being as interesting as we in fact are?

First, and most crucially, we bore when we lose faith that it really could be our feelings that would stand the best chance of interesting others. Out of modesty, and habit, we push some of our most interesting perceptions to one side in order to follow respectable but dead conventions of what might impress. When we tell anecdotes, we throw the emphasis on the outward details—who was there, when we went, what the temperature was like— rather than maintaining our nerve to report on the layer of feelings beneath the facts: the moment of guilt, the sudden sexual attraction, the humiliating sulk, the career crisis, the strange euphoria at 3 a.m.

Our neglect of our native feelings isn't just an oversight; it can be a deliberate strategy to keep our minds away from realizations that threaten our ideas of dignity and normality. We babble inconsequentially to the world because we lack the nerve to look more closely and unflinchingly within.

It feels significant that most 5-year-olds are far less boring than most 45-year-olds. What makes children gripping is not so much that they have more interesting feelings than anyone else, but that they are uncensored correspondents of these feelings. Their inexperience of the world means they are still instinctively loyal to themselves; they will candidly tell us what they really think about granny and their brother, what their plans for reforming the planet are and what they believe everyone should do with their boogers. We are rendered boring not by nature so much as by a fateful will—that begins its malevolent reign over us in adolescence—to appear normal.

Even when we are honest about our feelings, we may still prove boring because we don't know them as well as we should, and so get stuck at the level of insisting on an emotion rather than explaining it. We'll assert—with ever-greater emphasis—that a situation was "exciting," "awful" or "beautiful" but not be able to provide those around us with any of the sort of related details and examples that would help them viscerally understand why. We can end up boring not so much because we don't want to share our lives as because we don't yet know them well enough to do so.

Fortunately, the gift of being interesting is neither exclusive nor reliant on exceptional talent; it requires only direction, honesty, and focus. The person we call interesting is in essence someone alive to what we all deeply want from social intercourse: an uncensored glimpse of what the brief waking dream called life looks like through the eyes of another person and reassurance that we are not entirely alone with all that feels most bewildering, peculiar, and intense within us.

xi.
How to Talk about Yourself

Polite people have it instilled in them from an early age that they should not talk too much about themselves. A few comments aside, they should—to prove appealing—always ask the other about their lives or stick to impersonal topics found in newspapers, lest they be accused of the heinous charge of self-absorption.

But this rule fails to distinguish between different ways of talking about oneself. There are, as well-mannered people sometimes forget, better and worse ways to share details of one's life. It is not the amount that one talks that should determine the issue, only how one does so.

There is one particular way of discussing oneself that, however long it goes on for, never fails to win one friends, reassure audiences, comfort couples, bring solace to the single, and buy one the goodwill of enemies: the confession of vulnerability and error. To hear that we have failed, that we are sad, that it was our fault, that our partners don't seem to like us much, that we are lonely, that we have wished it might all be over—there is scarcely anything nicer anyone could learn.

This is often taken to signal a basic nastiness in human nature, but the truth is more poignant. We are not so much crowing when we hear of failure as deeply reassured—reassured to know that we aren't humiliatingly alone with the appalling difficulties of being alive. It is all too easy to suspect that we have been uniquely cursed in the extent of our troubles, of which we seldom find evidence in the lives around us. The media offers us unending accounts of the financial and creative success of others, while our friends and acquaintances constantly pepper their conversations with ever so subtle boasts about their and their children's accomplishments.

By an ultimate irony, these self-promoters aren't trying to alienate us. They are laboring under the touching but misguided impression that we will like them more for their success. They are applying to social life a model of a relationship between popularity and success that only applies in very selective contexts—perhaps when we seek to please our parents or need the help of successful people to advance our careers. But the rest of the time, as the boasters forget, we find success an enormous problem.

We put in so much effort to be perfect. But the irony is that it's failure that charms, because others so need to hear external evidence of problems with which we are all too lonely: how un-normal our sex lives are; how misguided our careers are proving; how unsatisfactory our family can be; how worried we are pretty much all the time.

Revealing any of these wounds might, of course, place us in great danger. Others could laugh; social media could have a field day. That's the point. We get close by revealing things that would, in the wrong hands, be capable of inflicting humiliation on us. Friendship is the dividend of gratitude that flows from an acknowledgment that one has offered something very valuable to someone by talking: not a fancy present, but something even more precious, the key to one's self-esteem and dignity. It's deeply poignant that we should expend so much effort on trying to look strong before the world, when it's only ever the revelation of the somewhat embarrassing, sad, melancholy, and anxious parts of us that is what makes us endearing to others, and transforms strangers into friends.

xii.
How Not to Rant

One of the risks of social life is that we will in the course of an evening or in the kitchen at a party end up trapped with a person of excessive conviction—or, to put it more colloquially, a bore. Bores can be found harboring any manner of obsessions: They may be deeply concerned about grammar (and the ever-increasing misuse of the subjunctive) or believe that modern architecture has alienated us from ourselves; they may be horrified by the predatory nature of contemporary capitalism or disgusted by the whingeing of the environmental movement; they might hate feminism or see misogyny in every corner of life. Bores aren't necessarily misguided (they may make some good points along the way), but our discomfort in their company arises from the intensity and relentlessness of their manner. We long for them to fall silent and give us the chance to run away.

Part of the reason why bores bore is that we sense they are not being entirely honest with us. They are certainly upset, but the real reasons why don't seem on offer. We feel—in the midst of their explanations—that their intensity is drawing heat from a source beyond the argument as they define it. They may be emphasizing a range of studiously impersonal political, economic, or social factors, but we intuit that there must be a more personal story from which we, and their conscious selves, have been carefully shielded.

It's a general truth, in no way humiliating, that our seemingly objective adult concerns often have their roots in incidents of personal vulnerability that unfolded long ago and that may be awkward to recover and discuss. Perhaps, when we were young, our father lost his job to a corporation that relocated their offices to southeast Asia: the pay-off was relatively generous but the shame intense for the family. Or perhaps we have been passed over for promotion many times by a young and conspicuously fashionable management team with an interest in contemporary design. Or maybe there was once a woman we liked very much, who was doing a PhD in gender studies on the work of Julia Kristeva and who showed signs of interest but then went off with a rival. These things upset us for a while. We may not like to remember these incidents, let alone tell new acquaintances about them at parties, yet they are still active within us and seek some way, however disguised, of expressing themselves. But all we know consciously is that capitalism is the most abusive and unsustainable economic system ever devised; that modern architecture has shamefully forgotten the nobility of the Classical tradition as embodied by the works of Bramante and Schinkel; and that feminists are out to systematically destroy the foundations of male earning power in advanced economies.

When we come across such ardent views, it isn't that we want to hear less, it's that we would ideally want to hear more, but in another direction: inwards, rather than further into sociocultural and economic abstractions. We want to do this not from prurience but because social life is guided by a wish to encounter the reality of other people, which is here being arcanely denied. Our boredom is at base an impatient resentment at being held at bay from the genuine traumas of another's life.

The bore is never just other people. It is—in given areas—also us. When we take a psychological audit of our intellectual ideas, we all stand to discover that some of our concerns owe their intensity to personal experiences that are hard to define and frightening to own up to.

This alerts us to how we might in the future respond to the speeches of the over-zealous. The task is not to engage head-on with the matter apparently at stake; it's to gently try to shift the conversation away from its official target to its origins, sympathetically asking when the issue first emerged and what more personal associations might surround it.

Even if we never get there, the knowledge of the structure of the problem should make us careful not to engage people of excessive conviction in too many prolonged head-to-head arguments. There is no point trying to list why capitalism is not the worst system ever devised, why modern architecture has its high points and why feminism remains necessary. This would be to believe that the other's rage was a kind of intellectual error that could be magically resolved with the help of one or two deft ideas. The kind conversationalist is more compassionately pessimistic. They accept that the roots of certain of our convictions lie deeply tangled in frightened, anxious parts of the psyche unlikely to be accessible outside psychotherapy.

We're so aware that it could sound patronizing to treat people as less self-aware than they believe themselves to be, we overlook that it may actually be generous to keep in mind the complicated role that denied personal wounds play in our ardent convictions. And we should hope that others will repay us the favor the next time we find ourselves delivering long and ever more intense speeches about the decline in handshaking, the colonization of Ecuador, or the corruption of the English language.

xiii.
The Charm of Vulnerability

The desire to fit in is deeply ingrained in our nature. We are social creatures with a long evolutionary history that stressed the importance of not standing out in a group. The oddball would be the last to get their share of mammoth meat. We are the descendants of those who conformed—and got fed.

It is understandable if we become awkward, and very lonely, around our own oddities. We become reluctant to admit to anything very strange about ourselves. We police our admissions and strive to appear more usual than we really are. We might say we like football because it feels difficult, as a man, to admit to much else. We feel constrained to order a whiskey at the bar because it would be very confusing to confess to one's real desire: a glass of milk. Perhaps we are among the handful of adults who are interested in toy trains and have joined a society to find out more; maybe we find wearing an old-fashioned watch enhances the intensity of our lovemaking; perhaps on vacation we secretly like to visit local hydrochemical plants. Our oddities can be intensified when other aspects of our lives are taken into account. If we are a tax-specialist director of a law firm, it is especially awkward to announce an interest in socialism. If we are studying engineering, it can be tricky to reveal to fellow students that ideally we would like to be a puppet maker; if we are a flight attendant, our colleagues might take it badly if we discussed at any length our admiration for the novels of Benjamin Disraeli.

It is this background of secrecy that explains our delight when, finally, someone dares publicly to be a bit strange: when they say, for example, that they are sexually turned on by sports cars or the Russian president or are so phobic about germs they always open public bathroom doors with their feet; when they tell us— with no particular embarrassment—that they spent the weekend crying at how badly their careers have gone or are engaged in an online flirtation with someone almost twice their age on another continent.

It isn't that we necessarily share these habits and interests. The delight such comments can provoke lies in the permission they give us to bring our own more curious sides to the fore. The confidence of the confessor encourages us to feel more at ease with our specific range of disavowed feelings. Via their simultaneous awareness of their oddity and their ease with it, they are establishing a possibility that we too could make use of around our quirks. In their courage to speak, they are operating with a more accurate and more consoling picture of human nature: one alive to the fact that—statistically speaking— we are all bizarre in quite a few respects. It is extremely normal to be rather abnormal.

The confident confessor is sure we all do equally odd (but very different) things. These unusual things, they suggest, are highly compatible with being a pleasant person deserving of love. Through their cheerful acceptance of their own strangeness, they break the oppressive link between being similar and being thought nice, which is otherwise so often active as a punitive force in our minds.

Charming frankness isn't merely engaging to encounter; it is a guide to our own less lonely future.

xiv.
The Ultimate Test of Your Social Skills

It can be easy to imagine that we possess reasonable social skills, because we know how to maintain conversation with strangers and—every now and then—manage to make a whole table laugh.

But there's a test far sterner than this, surprising in its ability to trip us up: the challenge of having a pleasant time with a child we don't know. Theoretically speaking, this should be easy. We were all kids once. We know a great deal more than they do and—as far as they're concerned—hold all the cards: If we felt like it, we could buy 26 packets of cookies and go to bed whenever we wanted.

Yet, in reality, it is strangely hard to feel at ease around children we're not already close to. Imagine being invited around to your boss's house for lunch and being left alone at the kitchen island with her moody 10-year-old son, or being introduced into a playroom with two shy 5-year-old girls, the children of a friend. We may swiftly become bewilderingly tongue-tied and inept.

The reason is that children are unable to do any of the normal things that ease social encounters between adult strangers. They don't ask polite questions about what we've been up to. They have no feeling for our lives or what might be important to us. They don't talk about the news or the weather. They can't usually tell us much about themselves and their enthusiasms. If we ask them why they like a toy or a movie, they tend to look blank and say they just like it, that's all.

So, for all their sweetness, children present formidable and fascinating barriers to social fluidity—which is also why they are the greatest tests of one's mastery of the arts of charm and kindness.

Across cultural history we have a few moving examples of accomplished adults getting on well with children. The French philosopher Michel de Montaigne (1533–1592) remarked that he found "nothing more notable" in the life of Socrates (the man who more or less began Western philosophy) than that he was exceptionally gifted at playing with children, and would, especially in his later years, spend many hours playing games and giving them piggy-backs. "And it suited him well," added Montaigne, "for all actions, says philosophy, equally become and equally honour a wise man."

Henri IV, king of France from 1589 to 1610, is remembered as one of the most benign French monarchs who also happened to be very sweet around children. On one occasion, famously painted by Ingres (recreating the scene two centuries after its occurrence), the Spanish ambassador came to see the king and found him pretending to be a horse for his children to ride on. Rather than interrupt the game immediately, Henri kept the ambassador waiting a little while, sending out

Jean-Auguste-Dominique Ingres, *Henry IV Surprised by the Spanish Ambassador While Playing with His Children*, 1817. Henri IV was one of the rare cases of a high-status adult who took care to cultivate kind and playful relationships with children.

a strong signal of where he felt sensible adult priorities should sometimes lie.

What is touching in these cases is that the adults did not insist on using their obvious, socially endorsed, strengths around children. Socrates did not opt to deliver lectures about metaphysics, and Henri IV did not sit impassively on a throne discussing how to rule a kingdom. They put aside their well-known virtues and prestige in order to make themselves vulnerable—as one must whenever friendship is at stake. They dared to lay themselves open to attack by those who might have described them as "silly" or "undignified," implicitly understanding that friendship can only emerge when we let the fragile, unadorned parts of us meet without artifice the fragile, unadorned parts of others.

Furthermore, these two grand men knew how to find common ground with creatures who were, in so many respects, entirely alien to them. Cosmopolitans of the mind, they imaginatively searched for what unites rather than what divides people and were able to locate, somewhere within their characters, the joys and excitements of someone who has only been on the earth a few years.

The socially adept know that we contain (even if only in trace, embryonic forms) all human possibilities within us, which they draw upon to feel their way into the needs and points of view of strangers. Even if they happen to be confident, they will know how to be in touch with the more timid version of themselves; even if they are financially secure, they can mobilize their own experience of anxiety to enter the inner world of someone beset by money worries; even if their careers have not gone well, they can, without bitterness, find a part of themselves that would love to prosper and use this to engage warmly with someone whose professional life has gone very well indeed.

The moves that these grand people made with children are ones we should all learn how to make with anyone, of whatever age, who we want to bond with. But it is particularly useful that these were grand people who made neighing sounds, for what so often holds us back around others, and makes us cold when we deep down long to be close, is a fear of a loss of dignity. Friendship begins, and loneliness can end, when we cease trying to impress, have the courage to step outside our safety zones and can dare, for a time, to look a little ridiculous.

Picture credits

Cover   Maskot / Getty Images

p. 112   Christen Købke, *View of Dosseringen, Copenhagen, with Willows in the Foreground*, c. 1837. Photo: Pernille Klemp

p. 131   Jean-Auguste-Dominique Ingres, *Henry IV Surprised by the Spanish Ambassador While Playing with His Children*, 1817. Musée des Beaux-Arts de la Ville de Paris, Petit Palais. Credit: Roger-Viollet / Topfoto

Also available from The School of Life:

The School of Life: Calm

The harmony and serenity we crave

A guide to developing the art of finding serenity by understanding the sources of our anxiety and frustrations.

Nowadays almost all of us wish we could be calmer; it is one of the distinctive longings of the modern age. Across history people have sought adventure and excitement, however a new priority for many of us is a desire to be more tranquil. This is a book designed to support us in our endeavors to remain calm against all the adversities life throws at us.

A calm state of mind is not a divine gift, we can alter our responses to everyday things and educate ourselves in the art of remaining calm, not through slow breathing or special teas, but through thinking.

This is a book that explores the causes of our greatest stresses and anxieties and gives us a succession of highly persuasive, beautiful, and sometimes dryly comic arguments with which to defend ourselves against panic and confusion.

ISBN: 978-1-915087-14-0
£9.99 | $14.99

THE SCHOOL OF LIFE

RELATIONSHIPS

Learning to love

The School of Life: Relationships

Learning to love

A book to inspire closeness and connection, helping people not only to find love but to make it last.

Few things promise us greater happiness than our relationships—yet few things more reliably deliver misery and frustration.

Our error is to suppose that we are born knowing how to love and that managing a relationship might therefore be intuitive and easy. This book starts from a different premise: that love is a skill to be learnt, rather than just an emotion to be felt.

It calmly and charmingly takes us around the key issues of relationships, from arguments to sex, forgiveness to communication, making sure that success in love need never again be just a matter of luck.

ISBN: 978-1-915087-13-3

£9.99 | $14.99

THE SCHOOL OF LIFE

SMALL PLEASURES

What makes life truly valuable

The School of Life: Small Pleasures

What makes life truly valuable

Explores and appreciates the small pleasures found in everyday life.

So often we exhaust ourselves and the planet in a search for very large pleasures, while all around us lies a wealth of small pleasures, which if only we paid more attention could bring us solace and joy at little cost and effort. But we need some encouragement to focus our gaze.

This is a book to guide us to the best of life's small pleasures: the distinctive delight of holding a child's hand, having a warm bath, the joy of the evening sky. It is an intriguing, evocative mix of small pleasures to heighten the senses and return us to the world with new-found excitement and enthusiasm.

Small pleasures turn out not to be small at all: they are points of access to the great themes of our lives. Every chapter puts one such moment of enjoyment under a magnifying glass to find out what's really going on in it and why it touches and moves us and makes us smile.

ISBN: 978-1-915087-16-4
£9.99 | $14.99

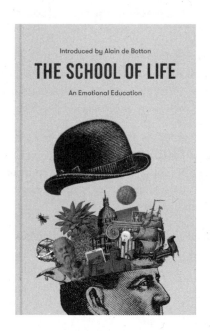

Introduced by Alain de Botton

THE SCHOOL OF LIFE

An Emotional Education

The School of Life: An Emotional Education

**How to live wisely and well in the twenty-first century—
an introduction to the modern art of emotional intelligence.**

Emotional intelligence affects every aspect of the way we live, from romantic to professional relationships, from our inner resilience to our social success. It is arguably the single most important skill for surviving the twenty-first century. But what does it really mean?

One decade ago, Alain de Botton founded The School of Life, an institute dedicated to understanding and improving our emotional intelligence. Now he presents the gathered wisdom of those ten years in a wide-ranging and innovative compendium of emotional intelligence which forms an introduction to The School of Life. Using his trademark mixture of analysis and anecdote, philosophical insight, and practical wisdom, he considers how we interact with each other and with ourselves, and how we can do so better.

From the reigning master of popular philosophy, *The School of Life: An Emotional Education* is an essential look at the skill set that defines our modern lives.

ISBN: 978-1-912891-45-0
£10.99 | $14.99

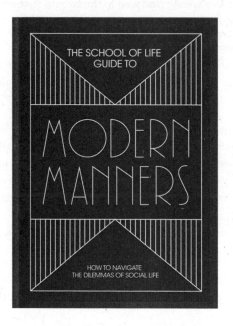

THE SCHOOL OF LIFE
GUIDE TO

MODERN MANNERS

HOW TO NAVIGATE
THE DILEMMAS OF SOCIAL LIFE

The School of Life Guide to Modern Manners

How to navigate the dilemmas of social life

This essential guide explores how etiquette is defined by consideration and respect, while putting good manners back at the center of our priorities.

Modern life is full of minor but acute dilemmas: wishing to end a boring conversation without causing offense; forgetting a name when introducing friends; running into an ex on a first date with a new partner ...

Though they might seem insignificant, such dilemmas illustrate some of the greatest themes in social existence: how to pursue our own happiness while honoring the sensitivities of others; how to convey goodwill with sincerity; and how to be kind without being supine or sentimental.

This book puts good manners back at the center of our lives. Through twenty case studies, *Modern Manners* provides a new philosophy of graceful conduct. Far from trivial diversions, manners are the practical expression of a dignified mission to create a kinder and more considerate world.

ISBN: 978-1-912891-14-6
£12 | $16.99

HOW TO
FIND THE RIGHT
WORDS

A GUIDE TO DELIVERING
LIFE'S MOST AWKWARD MESSAGES

The School of Life

How to Find the Right Words

A guide to delivering life's most awkward messages

Twenty case studies explaining how to gently deliver a range of life's most difficult messages while causing minimal harm.

Life constantly requires us to give other people some hugely awkward messages: that we don't love them anymore; that we do love them (though we're not meant to); that they smell a bit; that they're fired; that we're furious with them (though we adore them); or that their music is too loud ...

Often, out of embarrassment, we just stay quiet. Occasionally we explode. And, typically, we stumble about, looking for the right words – dreading that we didn't find them and thereby causing more hurt than we should.

This is a book to help us locate the best possible words to get across a range of life's most difficult messages. In 20 case studies drawn from relationships, friendships, work, our families, and interactions with strangers, we are gently shown what we might—in an ideal world—find ourselves saying to make our intentions known while causing minimal harm.

ISBN: 978-1-912891-51-1
£12 | $16.99

THE SCHOOL OF LIFE
A More Loving World
How to increase compassion, kindness and joy

A More Loving World

How to increase compassion, kindness, and joy

**A book to encourage compassion and forgiveness, showing us
how we can work towards a better and kinder world.**

The modern world is richer, safer, and more connected than ever before
but it is—arguably—also a far less loving world than we need or want:
impatience, self-righteousness, moralism, and viciousness are rife,
while forgiveness, tolerance, and sympathetic good humor can be in
short supply.

This is a book that rallies us to remember how much we all long for and
depend on love: how much we need people to forgive us for our errors,
how much everyone deserves to be treated with consideration and
imagination, and how being truly civilized means extending patience
and kindness to all those we have to deal with, even, and especially,
those who don't naturally appeal to us.

This book reminds us of our better natures and mobilizes us to fight for
the kinder, more loving world we essentially long for at heart.

ISBN: 978-1-912891-86-3
£12 | $16.99

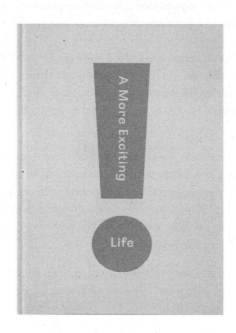

A More Exciting Life

A guide to greater freedom, spontaneity, and enjoyment

A guide to achieving the more joyful and interesting life that we know is within our grasp.

One of the things we all deeply crave, and all richly deserve, is a more exciting life. We know well enough that many things have to be routine, hard, and a little bit boring. But we also rightly sense that, if only we can find a way, our lives could be rendered intermittently more joyful, intense, thrilling, and beautiful.

This is a guide to the more exciting life we know could be ours. It isn't about the outward things we might do: travel, parachute out of airplanes or learn a foreign language. This is a book of psychology and about how we can nurture a sense of inner liberation, accept our desires and aspirations, and then have the courage to set ourselves free. Here is a guide to that more exciting life we know should—and can—be ours.

ISBN: 978-1-912891-25-2
£15 | $19.99

The School of Life is a global organization helping people lead more fulfilled lives. It is a resource for helping us understand ourselves, for improving our relationships, our careers and our social lives—as well as for helping us find calm and get more out of our leisure hours. We do this through films, workshops, books, apps, gifts, and community. You can find us online, in stores, and in welcoming spaces around the globe.